UNASHAMED

STUDY GUIDE

Also by Christine Caine

Unashamed (book)
Undaunted (book and video study)
Living Life Undaunted (365-day devotional)
Unstoppable

UNASHAMED

DROP THE BAGGAGE, PICK UP YOUR
FREEDOM, FULFILL YOUR DESTINY

STUDY GUIDE
FIVE SESSIONS

CHRISTINE CAINE

WRITTEN BY KEVIN AND SHERRY HARNEY

ZONDERVAN®

ZONDERVAN

Unashamed Study Guide
Copyright © 2016 by Christine Caine

This title is also available as a Zondervan ebook.

Requests for information should be addressed to:
Zondervan, 3900 *Sparks Dr. SE, Grand Rapids, Michigan 49546*

ISBN 978-0-310-69848-7

Published in association with the literary agency of David O. Middlebrook, 4501 Merlot Avenue, Grapevine, Texas 76051.

Cover design: Jessica Davis
Cover photography: David Dobson Photography
Interior design: Kait Lamphere

First Printing May 2016 / Printed in the United States of America

CONTENTS

OF NOTE

The quotations interspersed throughout this study guide and the introductory comments are excerpts from the book *Unashamed* and the video-based curriculum of the same name by Christine Caine. All other resources—including the small group questions, session introductions, and between-sessions materials—have been written by Kevin and Sherry Harney in collaboration with Christine Caine.

A WORD FROM CHRISTINE CAINE

I spent the first twenty-two years of my life shackled by shame. Looking back, I realize I had always felt it. It had been a part of my life from my earliest memories.

I felt it when I was rejected. Made to feel unworthy. Of no value.

I felt it when I was abused. And couldn't tell anyone. And believed it was somehow my fault.

I felt it when I tried to hide who I was, apologize for who I was, minimize my talents, or overachieve and compensate for feeling somehow "less than."

Have you felt it? If you're human, you have—and the result is always the same.

Shame makes us feel small. Flawed. Not good enough. And controlled.

Shame is the fear of being unworthy, and it adversely affects our relationship with God, others, and ourselves. It greatly hinders our ability to receive God's unconditional love—and share it with others.

Because of God's great love, I began to discover the power of God's Word to break through the lies I had believed—and to reveal the truth of who I am and why I was created. Breaking free from the shackles of shame is not an overnight experience or a quick-fix, ten-step process. It is, however, a grand, ongoing adventure of discovering the depths of God's love and the huge scope of God's power to transform us, re-create us, and continually renew us. This process will not end until we meet him face to face.

The development of this curriculum, along with the writing of the book *Unashamed,* is yet another step in my journey. I pray that my story and this study will open your heart and allow God to lift the shame off you so you can flourish and become all that he has created you to be.

Do you struggle with the fear that you are not enough?

Are you afraid to let your true self be seen and known?

Are you always trying to gain approval? Trying to prove you are valuable and worthy to be loved?

Do you want to break the power of shame in your life?

If so, join me and your small group members as we learn to drop the baggage of shame, pick up our freedom in Christ, and step into the fullness of the destiny—the shame-free life—God has in store for us.

I pray that these five sessions of learning, and the exercises you will do between the sessions, will help you take the next steps on your journey to freedom. As you read, the enemy will be trembling, because he knows that once God has broken the chains of our slavery to shame, there will be no holding us back!

God created you for a unique purpose. He has a specific plan for your life, and he has a powerful destiny he wants you to fulfill. And guess what? Shame has no place in that purpose, plan, and destiny. Jesus came to set you free from shame.

"It is for freedom that Christ has set us free. Stand firm, then, and do not let yourselves be burdened again by a yoke of slavery" (Galatians 5:1).

Session 1

RUN, DON'T HIDE

Introduction

Anna went to the doctor for a routine checkup and some additional "age appropriate" tests. At forty, she had been super healthy all her life. As a matter of fact, she had never had a broken bone, a surgery, or even a cavity. When she spoke of her good health, she would often say, "I guess I just have good genes!" When the doctor's office called two weeks later, she was shocked to learn of a number of serious concerns, including the possibility of cancer. She was given the number of a specialist to contact immediately. Two months later, Anna had still not told her husband and children about the doctor's report, and she had not yet called the specialist her doctor had recommended.

Simon was a curious eight-year-old boy. He loved to play, explore, and experiment with anything and everything . . . including fire. He found a pack of matches and went out into a field near his home to see if he could light them and start a "little campfire." In the dry summer conditions, starting a little fire was easy; the hard part was keeping it little. In less than sixty seconds, Simon's experiment had gotten out of control. He ran home as fast as he could. Instead of telling his parents, he hid in his bedroom. He did not want anyone to know what he had done.

Ricardo and Maria could see that their daughter was not the same happy, joy-filled young woman she had been two or three years ago. At seventeen she had become sullen, a recluse who stayed in her room most of the day. She rarely smiled and had very little to say. They did not want to intrude or seem overly concerned, so they decided to leave her alone and hope she figured things out on her own.

God always runs toward us, not from us.

Talk About It

Think about one of the three scenarios in the session introduction and tell about how this story might end if the pattern of running away were to continue.

or

How might the same story end on a happier, healthier note if there were a decision to run to the right person and address the challenge at hand?

You were created on purpose for a purpose.

Video Teaching

Watch the video teaching segment for session one, using the following outline to record anything that stands out to you.

Notes

There is ice cream on your face

The life-giving balance of grace and discipline

The difference between "who" and "do"

Many women have been trained to live in shame:

Shame we put on ourselves . . .

Shame others impose on us . . .

The shame-lifting story of a loving Father

The only antidote to the power of shame . . . the unconditional love, grace, and acceptance of God revealed in Jesus:

The difference between shame and guilt

We are loved, accepted, and sons and daughters of the King of kings

Get up and run to the Father, not away from him

 Shame tries to keep us hiding from God rather than running to God.

Video Discussion and Bible Study

1. Tell about a time you got caught doing wrong but were afraid to admit it. Why do you think we tend to run away and hide instead of quickly admitting our wrong?

2. Nick and Christine still disciplined their daughter Sophia after she admitted her wrong and expressed genuine sorrow. How is this kind of discipline actually a sign of deep love and devotion? How does God extend grace to us and yet still lovingly discipline us?

3. How does realizing that our "who" and our "do" are not the same become the starting point of freedom from shame that wants to keep us imprisoned and shackled to our past?

 A lot of times we feel such shame that we never recover from what we did because we cannot separate our "who" from our "do."

4. Christine shares honestly about the shame she lived with and carried deep in her soul for many years. She also talked about how most women deal with some kind of shame in their lives. Take a moment to reflect on some of the sources of shame that can keep a person shackled, unable to fully receive God's love, and unable to pursue his vision for their lives. Identify one or more of these that seems to be alive and working in your life:

- Shame over what someone has done to you in the past

- Shame over some aspect of your physical appearance

- Shame over needing the help of others and feeling you are not strong enough

- Shame over a poor and ungodly decision in the past

- Shame over how you parent (as you compare yourself to other parents and families)

- Shame over your personality and fundamental wiring as a person

- Shame over your dreams, hopes, and aspirations

- Shame over something else

Silently pray for God to give you courage and strength to face this shame and to bring it, in a new way, to the foot of the cross of Jesus. For those who feel led, tell the others in your group about one source of shame in your life. Seek to explain, as best you can, how this shame is affecting you.

 The perfect antidote to shame is the unconditional love, grace, and acceptance of Jesus toward each and every one of us.

5. **Read** Psalm 139:1–14. King David, the person inspired by the Holy Spirit to write this beautiful prayer, knew a lot about shame (self-imposed shame as well as shame placed on him by others). Yet he could write this bold declaration about himself and the God he loved. What do you learn from David's perspective in this psalm?

Describe a time you actually felt wonderfully loved and accepted in the eyes of God. How does knowing and embracing God's amazing love change how you see yourself?

Nothing that you have done can change the fact that you are created in the image of God. You are a son or daughter of the King of kings and the Lord of lords.

6. **Read** Luke 15:11–24. The father in this parable is a picture of God, your heavenly Father. The wandering and rebellious child is a picture of you and me. What do you learn about the love and heart of the Father in this beautiful story?

7. Christine makes an interesting and provocative declaration in today's session. She says that shame is destructive and demonic, but guilt can be valuable and helpful on our spiritual journey. What is the difference between shame and guilt? Why is it essential that we crush shame and still embrace the good aspects of guilt?

Jesus qualifies those whom the devil has tried to disqualify. He has borne your shame so that you no longer need to carry the burden of shame.

8. What does it mean to declare, "What we do can be wrong, but doing these things does not make *us* wrong"? How can admission of our wrong and guilt before God, and running to the cross of Jesus, lead to freedom from shame?

God declares that our "who" is far greater than our "do."

9. In the story of the rebellious and wandering son, there was a moment when the young man came to his senses, got up out of the pigpen, and began heading home to his father. This was the beginning of his healing process and freedom from shame. What will it look like for you to come to your senses, get up, and begin running toward God instead of away from him? Share specific ways you will need to change your thinking, attitude, actions, and lifestyle if you are going to seek freedom from shame.

*Only Jesus Christ can give us forgiveness
for our past. And here is the power
of it—a brand new life today.*

10. Respond to this statement, "If it is not revealed, it can't be healed!" Why is identifying our shame, admitting it, and sharing our story with other people essential in the freedom and healing process? How are you feeling about the coming four sessions of this *Unashamed* study?

How can your group members pray for you, encourage you, and support you in the coming week as you walk through this learning experience together?

*God can help you become a victor
and not a victim of your past.*

Closing Prayer

Spend time in your group praying in any of the following directions:

- Thank Jesus that he left the glory of heaven, bore your shame on the cross, and longs to set you free from all shame.

- Thank God that he not only extends amazing grace to you but also lovingly disciplines you because you are his precious child, whom he has fearfully and wonderfully made.

- Pray for eyes to see the spiritual reality that your "who" and your "do" are not the same.

- Pray for the members of your group to experience powerful freedom from shame in the coming weeks as you walk through this study together.

- Invite the Holy Spirit to show you the places in your heart and life where shame is entrenched and secretly seeking to destroy you.

 God longs for us to run to him and not from him.

BETWEEN-SESSIONS PERSONAL STUDY

You are invited to further explore the themes of *Unashamed* by engaging in any or all of the following between-sessions activity options. Any time you invest will be well spent; let God use it to draw you closer to him. And, as time allows, share with the group what you are learning when you gather next.

Shame Hunt

Take time in the coming week to survey your life: your relationships, your thoughts, your motives and attitudes. Where is shame hiding? Where has it made a home in your heart? What is driving and growing your shame? Be honest and humble. Ask the Holy Spirit to give you eyes to see, even if seeing the shame in your life is painful. Write down two places of shame that you identify.

One place of shame I identified:

How is this shame impacting how I see myself?

How is this shame shaping how I relate with others?

How is this shame causing me to run from God and not toward him?

How might this shame poison and damage my life if I don't face it and deal with it?

Another place of shame I identified:

How is this shame impacting how I see myself?

How is this shame shaping how I relate with others?

How is this shame causing me to run from God and not toward him?

How might this shame poison and damage my life if I don't face it and deal with it?

 Shame makes us feel unworthy. We end up running from God instead of running to God. And we run from each other rather than helping one another.

Social Media Evaluation

Reflect on your engagement in the world of social media (or media in general). Commit to pay attention to what you view, what you share with others, and how this might be a source of shame.

What social media do you participate in?

How much time do you spend watching media (TV, movies, online)?

What are some of the primary messages you are receiving from viewing social media and other forms of media? (Write down five messages below.)

Message:

Message:

Message:

Message:

Message:

How might these messages be creating a place for shame to take root and impact your life?

> **Shame makes us feel unworthy,**
> **like we are not enough.**

If you have concerns about the messages you are receiving or sending through media, consider doing a media fast for a week—eliminating or cutting back as much as possible. See if this impacts you in a positive way. If you do this, share the results with your group when you meet for the next session.

Start Running

If you have been avoiding God because of an area of shame in your life, commit to run *to* God in the coming days and weeks. Choose one or more of the "Run to God" exercises from the checklist below, and then use the journal section or a separate notebook to write about what God is teaching you through the exercises you've chosen.

- ☐ **Run to God #1:** Make a decision to be with your group at every session of the *Unashamed* study, even when you feel tempted to avoid it because the process might be getting difficult for you.

- ☐ **Run to God #2:** Commit to attend church weekly while you are walking through this study and seek to engage your heart, mind, and body fully in worship, even when you might feel some measure of shame and unworthiness.

- ☐ **Run to God #3:** Read a portion of the Bible each day and invite the Holy Spirit to speak to you, teach you, and minister to you as you read.

- ☐ **Run to God #4:** Begin a journal in which you write down three prayers of praise each day: one for God's love, grace, and goodness; another for someone in your life who is a blessing and joy; and a third for something about who God has made you and what he wants to do in and through you as his beloved child.

- ☐ **Run to God #5:** Read Psalm 139 each day for the next week. Slow down and meditate on verses 13 and 14, and say them out loud. Thank God that you are fearfully and wonderfully made!

When that shadow of shame lurks in the corners of our hearts, it holds us back from the fullness of all that God has for us. . . . You can leave your guilt and your shame at the cross and you can move past your past.

Journal

Use the space provided below to write some reflections on any of the following topics:

- How have you experienced both the grace and discipline of God, and how has this combination revealed God's fatherly love for you?

- Where have you too closely connected who you are (your "who") with what you have done in the past, or what you are doing right now (your "do")? What consequences might result if you can't separate your "who" and "do" in this area of your life?

- When you think of honestly sharing your places of shame with God and the members of your group, what will get in the way and tempt you to keep running from God and the people in your life?

- What are some possible results if you stop running and really face your shame?

- What are some possible consequences if you keep running from your shame and refuse to face it?

_____

_____

_____

_____

_____

_____

_____

_____

_____

_____

_____

_____

_____

_____

_____

_____

_____

> *God can and does redeem anything,*
> *and he is able to turn all things around*
> *to work together for good.*

Recommended Reading

This week as you reflect on what God is teaching you through this session, read chapters 1–2 of *Unashamed* by Christine Caine. In preparation for your next session, you might want to read chapters 3–5.

Session 2

TODAY IS THE DAY

Introduction

Throughout history, people have tried to overcome darkness. Lanterns, candles, and campfires were the tools of choice for millennia. Then Humphry Davy, an English scientist, made the first electric light in the early 1800s. Although it was not an actual light bulb, Davy had stumbled onto something revolutionary.

About seven decades later, Thomas Edison experimented with thousands of different filaments and found out that a carbon filament enclosed in an oxygen-free glass bulb would glow for up to forty hours. With more experimentation, Edison was able to invent a bulb that would burn for up to 1,500 hours.

Why all of this effort? Why such diligent experimentation and countless hours in the lab? The answer is simple: to eradicate darkness and replace it with light. There is something in the human spirit that is drawn to light. No one wants to sit or live in the darkness. We are made to thrive and live in the light.

When it comes to shame, it is a dark place, and God wants to shine light into our darkness. But to battle shame, we often have to stop running away from it and face it. We must face the darkness of shame and actually run toward it.

Think about the setting sun. If we were to run from the sunset, with our back to it, the darkness will still overcome us—but we will spend more time running in the dark. However, if we turn, face the darkness, and run full-speed straight into it, we will actually pass through it and enter the light more quickly.

This is the case with shame. We must face the darkness and pain of our shame and run toward it. The longer we deny it and run away, the slower the healing will be. It seems radically counterintuitive, but the fastest way to overcome the darkness of shame is to face it and run headlong toward it, with Jesus at our side.

We can't change the past, but we can make some decisions today that will change the future.

Talk About It

Tell about a time you had to press through pain so you could come out the other side healthier. What would have happened if fear of the pain had kept you from pressing forward?

or

Tell about a time you avoided dealing with something tough in your life. What happened as you denied and avoided this issue?

We must all choose to embrace the pain of recovery today. Jesus did what he could on the cross, and now we must do what only we can do here on the earth.

Video Teaching

Watch the video teaching segment for session two, using the following outline to record anything that stands out to you.

Notes

Embracing the pain of recovery

Calculating the cost of holding on to our shame

Letting go of our "what ifs"

I'll stay here one more day . . . really?

Today, not tomorrow

The long-term pain of shame or the short-term pain of dealing with shame—you choose

The cost of holding on to our shame:

Shame won't let us receive love

Shame steals our joy

Shame makes us settle for less than we deserve

Shame thrusts us into destructive tendencies

Shame robs us of the abundant, purpose-driven, passionate life Jesus
has planned for us

The path to a shame-free life

 Shame steals, kills, and destroys our purpose, our passion, and our potential.

Video Discussion and Bible Study

1. Christine teaches that many people never find healing from shame because they are afraid to face the pain. What are some of the costs and consequences if we refuse to do the hard work of facing our shame and dealing with it? What are some consequences you have faced, or might face, because of shame in your life?

2. What are some things that can help us embrace the pain that comes with facing our shame and begin a process of moving forward and dealing with it . . . even when doing so is tremendously difficult?

There is no way you can move into the future if you stay focused on your past.

3. **Read** Exodus 8:1–15. Pharaoh, one of the most powerful people on the planet, actually decided to have Moses command the frogs to leave "tomorrow" and not "now, immediately, today!" What do you imagine Pharaoh was thinking when he made this request? What might have driven his decision to live in the misery of a frog-infested world for one more day?

What are some of the reasons you and I might decide to deal with the stench and mess of our shame "tomorrow" and not "now, immediately, today"?

Most people will carry yesterday's shame into today and tomorrow, unless they make a conscious decision to deal with it TODAY.

4. As strange as it might seem, a life saturated and ruled by shame can become familiar, comfortable, and predictable. We can get used to it. How can shame actually become something that we feel comfortable with (even while despising it)?

5. **Read** John 5:1–9. In this passage, Jesus encounters a man who has been ravaged by physical limitations for thirty-eight years. The man is waiting by a pool, where he hopes one day he will be healed. Yet when Jesus encounters this man, he asks him a question that seems quite strange. What was the question, and why do you think Jesus asked it?

6. Imagine you were to meet Jesus face-to-face today and he asked you, "Do you want to be healed from your shame?" What would you say to Jesus? How can the familiar pain we experience due to our shame seem safe and tame compared to the unknown journey we have to walk to overcome our shame?

 Jesus has set every one of us free, but it's up to us to decide to walk in that freedom.

7. One of the best ways to overcome shame is to look closely at the consequences of letting shame remain camped out in our hearts and lives. Respond to *one* of the following questions that most connects in your experience:

    - How has your shame kept you from fully experiencing God's love?

    - How has shame hindered you from receiving and embracing love from the people in your life?

    - How has shame gotten in the way of you loving other people with freedom and passion?

    - How has shame limited your capacity to experience and live in joy?

8. One consequence of buried shame in our lives is that it leads to hidden and destructive habits, including substance abuse, codependent relationships, self-harming, eating disorders, self-hate, and addictions (TV, shopping, social media, etc.). Share with your group (in confidence) one way that shame has led to a destructive pattern in your life. How can your group members pray for you and support you as you seek to reverse this pattern and live in a new place of health and freedom?

I have learned that in order to get unhooked from the pain of my past, I need to continuously choose to change my perspective. I need to look at things through God's eyes—through the resurrection power of Jesus Christ living on the inside of me.

9. **Read** Isaiah 53:1–7. This passage is a prophecy of what Jesus, the perfect Lamb of God, would do on the cross for us. What did Jesus do to bear our sins and destroy our shame? How should his willingness to suffer for us (to destroy our shame) motivate us to face the pain of dealing with our shame?

Jesus shamed our shame on the cross at Calvary.

10. If you follow Jesus on a journey toward the darkness of your shame, through it, and out the other side, what good and beautiful thing might God do in and through your life? Share a dream you have had about how God might use you and allow your group members to pray for this dream to become a reality as you are freed from shame.

"Instead of their shame, my people will receive a double portion, and instead of disgrace they will rejoice in their inheritance; and so they will inherit a double portion in their land, and everlasting joy will be theirs" (Isaiah 61:7, author paraphrase).

Closing Prayer

Spend time in your group praying in any of the following directions:

- Thank God for his patience with you, even when you have held on to shame rather than bringing it to the foot of the cross.

- Ask for courage to see and acknowledge where shame still has roots in your heart and life.

- Confess an area in your life where holding on to shame has led to bad consequences and pray for the grace of Jesus to cascade over your life, reminding you that you are loved and precious to him.

- Declare to God before your group members that today is the day you will face and deal with your shame, not tomorrow!

- Ask God to unleash his love, joy, and dreams in new and powerful ways as you walk away from shame and toward his plan for your life.

- Thank Jesus for bearing your shame on the cross.

 Jesus is fighting for you from a place of victory, not for victory.

BETWEEN-SESSIONS PERSONAL STUDY

You are invited to further explore the themes of *Unashamed* by engaging in any or all of the following between-sessions activity options. Any time you invest will be well spent; let God use it to draw you closer to him. And, as time allows, share with the group what you are learning when you gather next.

Counting the Cost

We pay a price when we continue to harbor shame in our lives. We may not even realize how great the cost unless we stop to evaluate the damage. On the flip side, we may not fully realize the blessings we would gain should the shame be lifted. Use this exercise to assess both.

Identify a specific area of shame in your life, one that bothers you most:

Next, list the consequences you have faced because of the power of shame in this specific area of your life:

Next, list possible or probable future consequences (for yourself and those you love) if you do not deal with this shame:

Now, list good and beautiful things that could enter your life if this shame were removed and you were truly set free from bondage to it:

Write down your thoughts about why you would hold on to your shame, or why you would face it and commit to deal with it:

Pray to God with humble passion and ask for courage to face your shame, bring it to the foot of the cross, and let God heal you and transform your past and your future. Journal your prayer below:

If this has been a helpful and clarifying process for you, use it to assess other areas of shame in your life.

 There is no such thing as a drive-through breakthrough.

Declare It!

Take time to write a series of brief but passionate declarations about your shame and your desire to be free from its hold. Be clear, starting this moment, that you are going to war with shame. You will not wait until tomorrow, or even an hour—you are starting this second. Now!

First, write a declaration to **God** the Father, in the name of Jesus the only Son, in the power of the Holy Spirit.

God Almighty, in your powerful name I come and declare that I am ready to leave shame behind. This is my prayer . . .

Next, write a declaration to **yourself**, stating your intention to go to war with shame, side-by-side with the great shame lifter, Jesus!

I make a commitment to myself, as a child of the living God, that I will no longer be a slave of shame. This is my commitment . . .

Finally, write a declaration to your **children** or **grandchildren** (living or future), stating your commitment to battle shame and not pass on a legacy of shame-filled behavior and attitudes to those who come after you.

I commit to the family members who will come after me, I know the poison of shame and I will not pass on my patterns of shame to you. This is my commitment to you . . .

 The fact is that the decision you make today to move from shame-filled to shame-free living doesn't only impact you; it impacts the generations that are to come after you.

Do I Ever Say "Tomorrow"?

Take time to humbly ask the Holy Spirit of God to search your heart. If you are still living with shame (and most of us are), then you can be confident there are ways you are saying, "Tomorrow!"

Choose a particular area of shame you struggle with and invite the Spirit of the living God, who loves you beyond description, to show you where and how you are holding on to it instead of dealing with it today.

Area of shame:

How I am holding on to it:

Why I am holding on to it:

What I need to do to begin dealing with this shame today:

 To become shame free, you first need to change your perspective. You need to choose to focus more on what Jesus has done for you, not what others have done to you.

Questions to Ponder

In this session, Christine asked some very provocative questions. Take time before your group meets next to think about each question. Then write down just a few sentences about how you would respond to each one.

How long will you stay stuck in what was?

How long will you accept what is instead of what could be?

How long will you allow the imagination of what might have been to rob you of the possibility of what could be?

How long will you spend not living the life you have because you are lamenting the life you had?

How long will you forsake your destiny because you are so fixated on your history?

Every one of us must decide to let
go of yesterday's what-ifs.

Journal

Use the space provided below to write some reflections on any of the following topics:

- What are the dreams and hopes God might unleash in your life if shame is driven out and the power of Jesus is unleashed in you?

- As you look back over your life and family history, what are some of the reasons and excuses that people in your family tend to use to justify not dealing with shame? How does this keep you and other family members stuck, unable to move forward in faith and life?

- If you have a place of secret behavior that is harmful to you and the people around you, what is it and how can God set you free from this as you face and deal with your shame?

_____

_____

_____

_____

_____

_____

_____

_____

_____

_____

_____

_____

_____

 Our history does not need to decide our destiny.

Recommended Reading

As you reflect on what God is teaching you through this session, read chapters 3–5 in *Unashamed* by Christine Caine if you haven't already. In preparation for your next session, you might want to read chapters 6–8.

Session 3

POSSESS YOUR INHERITANCE

Introduction

All of us have seasons of desert wandering. Like the people of Israel in the Old Testament, the Promised Land is right there in front of us, but we find ourselves in the wilderness. We would love to bypass it, but despite our best efforts there are no shortcuts.

The question is not, "Will I travel through the wilderness?" but, "How long will I stay there?" The truth is, the desert is not our home but simply a place from which we can move into God's plans, dreams, and desires for our lives. The wilderness is not our destination; it was never meant to be. God's desire is for us to march forward and onward . . . into his Promised Land.

Shame wants to consign us to a lifetime of wandering in arid and waterless places of emptiness, loneliness, fear, and hopelessness. Shame deceives us into believing that the desert is our destination, our home, exactly what we deserve. Shame whispers in our ear, "This is as good as it gets; you have earned this; get comfortable . . . you will never leave this place."

Jesus has other plans! He is the great shame lifter. He invites us to pack our bags and move out of the wilderness. He has good gifts waiting, blessings stored up, joy beyond our wildest dreams—a Promised Land that flows with milk and honey. What we need to do is make a decision to follow Jesus into his promises.

In *The Weight of Glory*, C. S. Lewis spoke of this idea with a powerful word picture: "We are half-hearted creatures, fooling around with drink and sex and ambition when infinite joy is offered us, like an ignorant child who wants to go on making mud pies in a slum because he cannot imagine what is meant by the offer of a holiday by the sea. We are far too easily pleased."

Too many of us have believed the lies of shame. We have become comfortable living in the slums of the wilderness. Into this desert land, Jesus comes and extends an invitation for us to follow him into the Promised Land. He offers us a holiday by the sea and calls us to infinite joy!

But there's a catch . . . he won't drag us in. He *invites* us in. Our part is to pack our bags and start walking away from shame into the future he has planned for us. When we do this, shame takes a lethal blow and a whole new life begins.

 The purpose of the Israelites' coming out of Egypt was to go into the Promised Land of Canaan. It wasn't to live in the wilderness.

Talk About It

What are some of the ways we settle for less than what God wants us to experience?

or

Tell about one way your life changed for the better when you became a follower of Jesus. How did your decision to follow the Savior propel you into a new life?

The truth is, that one moment, that one missed opportunity, that one mistake, that one failure doesn't need to define your life. Your life can be defined by a far more powerful moment, and that's the moment that Jesus Christ died on that cross.

Video Teaching

Watch the video teaching segment for session three, using the following outline to record anything that stands out to you.

Notes

A broken way of thinking: because I have experienced bad things, I must be a bad person

The difference between living delivered and living free

Decision time . . . will you take full possession of the land?

Some people never leave the wilderness and enter the Promised Land

We are freed from the bondage of Egypt and also freed to enter the Promised Land

Don't let one moment (or a series of moments) poison every other moment of your life

Bring your shame to the foot of the cross and leave your wandering in the desert as you enter God's Promised Land for your future

Will you take the short route or the long way to the Promised Land?

Trusting the trustworthy character of God

 You need to go through the wilderness to get into your Promised Land. But don't forget, Jesus is with you in the midst of the wilderness.

Video Discussion and Bible Study

1. Christine shares honestly about the many sources of shame she lived with before Jesus set her free. Over the past weeks, what sources of shame have you identified in your life? Have you noticed any changes as you have brought these into the light of Jesus?

> *Until we learn to trust God in the wilderness*
> *by exposing our baggage and allowing*
> *him to heal all of those broken places, we*
> *will never experience true freedom.*

2. What are some of the shame-driven recordings that have looped again and again in your mind through the years? Where do you think these messages came from? How have they impacted your life?

If you could play those recordings in the presence of the Savior who loves you and died on the cross to crush and destroy your shame, what would he say about the messages cycling through your mind? (Give specific responses you believe Jesus would give to specific lies that have been running through your heart for months, years, or even decades.)

3. **Read** Deuteronomy 8:1–9. What picture does God paint of the Promised Land in this passage (particularly the end of the passage)? What is God seeking to teach and inspire through this description? How is God painting a similar picture in your mind about the shame-free life he wants to lead you into?

It is in the wilderness season of our lives that God actually strengthens us and prepares us to overcome the inevitable giants that we are going to face in our Promised Land.

4. Christine explains that God's people embarked on an eleven-day journey that took them almost forty years to complete. Why did it take so long for God's people to travel such a short distance? How does shame cause us to become stuck in emotional deserts, relational deserts, spiritual deserts, addiction deserts, and others when God desires to lead us into his delight and Promised Land of blessing?

5. God's people were freed *from* slavery in Egypt. But they were also freed to enter into the Promised Land. What we learn in this passage is that they only embraced the first half of the freedom God offered. What does it look like when people today receive the freedom from sin that Jesus offers through his sacrifice on the cross, but they do *not* receive the freedom from shame? How is this only part of the freedom God wants to offer us?

Make no mistake, the people of Israel were always going to walk through a wilderness to get to the Promised Land, but it wasn't supposed to be a forty-year process.

6. God called the people to take possession of the land. They were expected to pack their bags, march in, and fight for their inheritance. Why do you think God called them to enter the process and do their part rather than simply handing them the land? Why do you think God calls you to battle shame, embrace his grace, and walk into his promises for you rather than just handing everything to you and making it easy?

7. Tell about an area of your life where you have been set free by Jesus, but you are still letting shame limit you and keep you from fully entering God's promises and desires for you.

 Shame-free living is definitely
not for the faint of heart.

8. Christine is clear that God expects us to enter this freedom process on every level. If you are going to fully follow God into his promises and purposes for your life, what changes will you need to make in *one or two* of these areas:

   • New ways of thinking of God

- New ways of seeing yourself

- New habits (and leaving old, bad habits)

- New ways of reacting when shame comes crashing in

- New ways of celebrating God's presence and power

- New ways of speaking to yourself

- New ways of treating others

9. Following is a list of typical patterns and signs that demonstrate when we are still living in the desert and not yet embracing God's gift of the Promised Land. How do you see some of these operating in your life and the lives of others who are under the power of shame?

- Being suspicious of people

- Second-guessing people

- Second-guessing yourself

- Seeking to control the people in your life

- Seeking to control your own life and the outcome of every situation

- Guarding your heart

- Never getting too close to people

- Performing for acceptance

- Perfectionism

- Running to addictions to cover pain

- Hiding and minimizing who you are

 It took one spectacular moment for the Lord to part the Red Sea and to take the slaves out of Egypt, but it would take a little while longer to take the slavery mentality out of the slaves!

10. **Read** Hebrews 12:1–3 and Matthew 27:45–46. There is a moment that can and should impact every other moment of our lives. It is when Jesus hung on a rugged wooden cross and bore our sins, pain, judgment, and shame. How can keeping our eyes and hearts fixed on Jesus, remembering his sacrifice for our sins and the power of his resurrection, help us turn from shame and move confidently toward God's will for our lives? How can that moment overcome and out-influence every moment of shame in our past?

If you are going to pack your things and move out of the desert of shame, what is one specific change you to need to make in the coming week? How will you begin on this journey? How can your group members pray for you, cheer you on, and support you?

It takes strength and courage to walk in freedom.

Closing Prayer

Spend time in your group praying in any of the following directions:

- Thank God that he has a shame-free Promised Land waiting for you. Ask him to help you see this good place and long to walk into it.

- Praise Jesus for taking your shame and opening the way for you to enter God's promises and plan for your future.

- Declare to God, in the power of the Holy Spirit, that you will no longer live in the wilderness of shame. Express your desire and commitment to pack your bags and move out of the desert.

- Praise your heavenly Father for being infinitely trustworthy, and ask him to help you live with trust and confidence in him at all times.

- Pray for specific members of your small group who have shared shame-filled areas they are trying to break through. Ask the Holy Spirit of God to set them free, empowering them to march confidently out of their wilderness of shame.

God's goal for us is freedom,
true spiritual freedom.

BETWEEN-SESSIONS PERSONAL STUDY

Renewing Your Mind

Meditate on and memorize Romans 12:1–2. Let the words of this passage and its Spirit-anointed themes permeate your heart and saturate your thinking:

Therefore, I urge you, brothers and sisters, in view of God's mercy, to offer your bodies as a living sacrifice, holy and pleasing to God—this is your true and proper worship. Do not conform to the pattern of this world, but be transformed by the renewing of your mind. Then you will be able to test and approve what God's will is—his good, pleasing and perfect will.

List some of the ways that shame-filled thinking has conformed you, your attitudes, and the way you see yourself, others, and God:

Now list ways you believe your mind needs to be renewed, rewired, and changed to reflect thinking that honors God:

> *There are so many people who get delivered from their situation, but they have never stepped into their spiritual Promised Land to partake of the fullness of God's promises.*

"Go-To" Shame-Buster Passages

Sometimes, as we walk through life, the power of shame seems to come at us with strong, consistent force. In these times, it is wise to have some "go-to" Bible passages to read, reflect on, and keep fresh in our hearts. Choose two or three of the following passages and put them in your phone, on a card in your purse or wallet, or in a file in your computer. When the battle against shame heats up, read them, think deeply about them, and believe them!

So if the Son sets you free, you will be free indeed. (John 8:36)

Therefore, there is now no condemnation for those who are in Christ Jesus. (Romans 8:1)

Bear with each other and forgive one another if any of you has a grievance against someone. Forgive as the Lord forgave you. (Colossians 3:13)

Therefore, holy brothers and sisters, who share in the heavenly calling, fix your thoughts on Jesus, whom we acknowledge as our apostle and high priest. (Hebrews 3:1)

Everyone who believes in him receives forgiveness of sins through his name. (Acts 10:43)

[Jesus] gave himself for us to redeem us from all wickedness and to purify for himself a people that are his very own, eager to do what is good. (Titus 2:14)

For you created my inmost being; you knit me together in my mother's womb. I praise you because I am fearfully and wonderfully made; your works are wonderful, I know that full well. (Psalm 139:13–14)

You will again have compassion on us; you will tread our sins underfoot and hurl all our iniquities into the depths of the sea. (Micah 7:19)

Praise the LORD, my soul, and forget not all his benefits—who forgives all your sins and heals all your diseases, who redeems your life from the pit and crowns you with love and compassion. (Psalm 103:2–4)

We have to allow God to replace the damaging repercussions of shame-filled living with the truth of his Word and his promises.

Nailing Shame to the Cross

We have all had experiences that unleashed shame in our hearts and lives. We need to take these one by one, name them, and bring them to the cross of Jesus. We need to realize that Jesus carried our shame, paid our price, and took our judgment. We do not need to carry these things any farther than the foot of the cross.

- Consider an area of shame you are still living with.

- Picture yourself carrying this experience, this pain, this memory to the cross of Jesus. Look up into his tear-stained face and remember why he died. Hear him say, "Father, forgive them, they do not know what they are doing!" Hear Jesus cry out, "It is finished!"

- Thank Jesus for covering your shame and cleansing your sin.

- Ask for power to leave your shame there at the cross, and never pick it up again.

You can choose today to go in and possess your freedom rather than keep circling that same old mountain of shame.

Dream a Big Dream

Christine shares about dreaming big dreams, even when she was a little girl. Ironically, she felt shame over dreaming such big dreams and believing she could do something extraordinary with her life. But through the years, God has taken those Holy-Spirit-initiated dreams and made them a reality.

1. In the coming week find a quiet place where you can pray and reflect for at least thirty minutes. Think back through your life (in particular your life as a follower of Jesus). What dreams has God birthed in your heart? They might seem silly, unattainable, and simply too big for you to comprehend, but write down two dreams you have had through the years:

Dream 1:

Dream 2:

2. Now think about what has shut down these dreams or kept you from pursuing them. How has shame, embarrassment, or limited thinking gotten in the way?

3. Devote time every day during this week to pray about these dreams. Not every dream is from God and not every dream from God needs to become a reality immediately. But if you sense this dream originated in the heart of God, don't let shame or personal limitations stand in the way.

4. Next, make a list of simple ways you could begin exploring what it would take to move each dream a step or two closer to reality.

Steps forward for Dream 1:

Steps forward for Dream 2:

5. Seek wisdom from godly friends and leaders about how to move forward and develop this vision in a way that will glorify Jesus and bless others.

Journal

Use the space provided below to write some reflections on any of the following topics:

- How has Jesus already freed you from some of your shame and led you into his Promised Land? Remember these great moments and the joy they bring as you look forward to experiencing more of them.

- Write down a few of the shame-driven recordings that seem to play over and over again in your heart and mind. What will it take for you to erase these recordings so that you don't have to hear these lies ever again?

- What are some of the indicators that you still have shame driving how you relate to others and how you see the world around you? How can you pay attention to these indicators so shame can't slip in and control your life again?

_____

_____

_____

_____

_____

_____

_____

_____

_____

_____

 You don't have to be totally fearless,
just more faithful.

Recommended Reading

As you reflect on what God is teaching you through this session, read chapters 6–8 of *Unashamed* by Christine Caine if you haven't already. In preparation for your next session, you might want to read chapters 9–10.

Session 4

GOD NEVER WASTES A HURT

Introduction

The more you read the Bible the more you realize that most of God's most faithful servants bore scars. Sometimes those scars were physical, while at other times they were emotional, relational, and even spiritual. Those scars were not there because of a lack of faith but because they followed the Lord closely. Jeremiah was thrown into a pit. Joseph was abandoned by his brothers and sold as a slave. David was ousted from Jerusalem by his own son. Daniel and his friends were prisoners of war. Esther was a stranger in a strange land and forced to marry the king. Ruth lost her husband. Hosea, the town prophet, watched as his wife abandoned him and went back to working as a prostitute. Stephen preached with passion and was stoned to death. The apostle Paul was strapped up at least five times and given forty lashes less one. He had 195 scars on his body for the sake of the gospel.

A quick survey of the Bible shows us a virtual parade of scar-covered saints who followed God faithfully, even when it meant they would suffer. So let's not expect life to bring us only smooth paths, sunny days, and a painless journey. Let's not be shocked when we face struggles from outside and even from within. Instead, let's commit to find our healing in Jesus. Let's allow the Savior to restore us. Let's commit to never hide our scars but let God use past pain to propel us to future glory . . . for the sake of Jesus.

Every scar tells a story. You can allow God to use your past to give someone else a future.

Talk About It

Tell about a time you were faithfully following Jesus and still faced pain, struggle, or hardship.

or

Tell about an encounter you had with a well-meaning Christian who tried to convince you that faithful followers of Jesus don't suffer or face hard times. What are some of the consequences if we buy into this misinformed theological disposition?

 God never wastes a hurt.

Video Teaching

Watch the video teaching segment for session four, using the following outline to record anything that stands out to you.

Notes

Facing battles in this life . . . we all do

In hard times, we must make choice after choice to trust Jesus and follow him

We always want to be "delivered from" but sometimes God calls us to "walk through"

Our scars can become a sign of victory and not defeat

Lessons from Joseph's journey into pain

God can bring good out of . . . anything

Beware of the bondage of bitterness

Release the baggage of unforgiveness

The "but God" factor

 Our scars can be a sign of victory and not defeat. They can become a source of hope instead of shame.

Video Discussion and Bible Study

1. Tell about a time that tragedy struck, bad news arrived, health waned, or heartbreak came your way. How did you see the enemy at work seeking to use this situation to discourage you? How has God used this hard time as an opportunity to grow you or bring glory to himself?

The enemy sends a spirit of fear to try to deactivate our faith and to try to paralyze and cripple us.

2. Christine talks about how we need to make the right choices in the middle of our struggles, pain, and suffering. Which of the following choices do you need to begin making as you face hard times, and how will you live out this choice?

- I choose to saturate my heart and mind in the truth of God's Word and not fixate on my struggle.

- I choose to look beyond the problem I face and focus on the victory that Jesus has already won.

- I choose to walk by faith and not by what my eyes can see.

- I choose to combat fear with faith in Jesus.

- I choose to surround myself with active prayer warriors rather than face this struggle alone.

- I choose to stay in Christian community and attend worship services regularly rather than be isolated and alone.

- I choose to guard my mouth and not speak words that are fear-filled, doubt-driven, negative, or faithless.

*If we want to pick up our freedom,
we have to be willing to drop the baggage.*

3. What is the difference between being delivered *from* something and walking *through* the same challenge in the presence and power of Jesus? How can each of these be honoring to God and bring him glory?

What are ways that God can use our journey through painful and hard times to grow our character, deepen our faith, and connect us more closely to each other?

4. **Read** Romans 8:28. The apostle Paul is clear that God can bring good out of any and all situations we face. This means that God can use our scars as a trophy of his miraculous power and amazing grace. Tell about one scar you have (physical, emotional, spiritual, or relational) and how this scar is now a testimony to the power, love, and glory of God.

Don't hide your scars; they are a trophy of the miracle-working power of the grace of God.

5. **Read** Genesis 50:15–21. As Christine summarized the story of Joseph and his brothers, it would seem that Joseph had every reason in the world to be bitter and vengeful. What do you learn about the heart and faith of Joseph in this passage?

6. Joseph's response was shockingly compassionate and beautifully gracious. We often do not respond kindly to those who have shamed and hurt us. Why are each of these responses difficult when others have hurt us deeply?

   • Joseph trusted God more than his human circumstances. What makes it hard for us to do this?

   • Joseph spoke words of kindness and compassion. Why is it so hard to speak well of those who have shamed and hurt us?

   • Joseph extended care and provision to those who had abandoned him. Why do we have a hard time extending tangible acts of kindness to the people who have intentionally hurt us?

- Joseph saw the bigger picture of God's plan and did not fixate on the specifics of his pain. What makes it challenging to see the good God can bring from our struggles and suffering?

Our wounds will only be mended when we let go of the bitterness and allow God to do what only he can do.

7. Think of a person who has shamed you, hurt you, or damaged your heart in some way. What word of blessing and kindness could you speak to this person? What act of graciousness could you extend?

How could you pray for God's hand, presence, and truth to penetrate this person's life? And how can your group members pray for you and encourage you as you learn to respond differently to those who have shamed you?

The key to forgiveness is to understand how much you and I have been forgiven by God.

8. Why is bitterness such a common (and understandable) condition of the heart when someone has hurt us and shamed us? What are some of the possible consequences we could live with if we allow bitterness to take root and rule our hearts? What steps can we take to dig out the roots of bitterness over past hurt?

9. **Read** Ephesians 4:31–32, Colossians 3:12–14, and Matthew 6:12, 14–15. Why do you think God takes forgiveness so seriously? How is the forgiveness we have received from the Father through the sacrifice of Jesus our perfect example?

Even when we know and have received the amazing grace of Jesus, it can be difficult to extend forgiveness generously and quickly to others. Why is it so hard for us to forgive others in the way we have been forgiven? Why are we afraid to forgive?

As God has taken leave of our sins in
Jesus, so we too should let go of the sins
that have been committed against us.

10. Christine talks about how often the Bible includes the phrase "but God." This is an indicator that someone did something hurtful or wrong, "but God" brought something good out of it. For example, Satan, the enemy of our soul, sought to destroy and kill, "but God" brought life and hope. Tell about a time in your life when hurt, pain, sorrow, and shame came crashing in, "but God" took this situation and brought good for you and glory for himself through that dark time.

Never underestimate the power
of "but God" in your life.

Closing Prayer

Spend time in your group praying in any of the following directions:

- Thank God for the times he has delivered you from deep pain and hurt. Also, thank him for the times he has walked with you through deep valleys of suffering and pain.

- Praise him for the good things he has brought out of your times of pain, loss, and struggle. Rejoice that he, and only he, can actually bring good out of the dark and painful times of life.

- Invite the Holy Spirit to use your scars and past pains as a testimony of his power to heal, his presence in the storms of life, and his ability to lead us out of the valleys we all walk through.

- Ask God to help you let go of bitterness and actually speak grace and extend care to those who have wronged you.

- Pray for eyes to see those "but God" moments when the Lord of glory has taken your scars and done an amazing work for his glory.

 Following Jesus does not end our pain, but it does transform it. Although God never causes our pain or shame, he can use it for our benefit, for his purposes, and to help other people.

BETWEEN-SESSIONS PERSONAL STUDY

Make a Choice

Christine talked about how when bad news came her way and her health was in jeopardy, she had to make choices that would orient her away from shame and discouragement and toward God. Think about an area of struggle, pain, or shame you are battling right now and commit to make wise choices that will honor God and propel you forward in your faith. Use the space below each choice or declaration to write a brief prayer. (And if you find this activity helpful, consider using the same prayer prompts to confront future struggles.)

Area of struggle, pain, or shame you are facing:

I choose to cover this problem with the promises of God. My prayer:

I choose to silence the giant of fear with biblical truth. My prayer:

I choose to see beyond the wall of my challenge to the victory on the other side. My prayer:

I choose to invite prayer warriors to support me and walk with me. My prayer:

I choose to saturate myself in the presence of God both privately and by staying connected in Christian community and worship times. My prayer:

I choose to read, believe, and follow the teaching of Scripture during this hard time rather than use my struggle as an excuse to avoid God's Word. My prayer:

I choose to silence fear, doubt, unbelief, and negativity. My prayer:

I choose to guard my confession and speak words of life rather than negative and hopeless words of death. My prayer:

Scar Study

Just as we bear physical scars of past injuries or surgeries, we bear scars from life's emotional wounds as well. Though they may not be visible, they are no less significant. Choose two scars on your "heart." Use the brief exercise below to help you identify where you are in the healing process:

My scar:

Where did this scar originate?

Is this scar still painful, or has it healed (so it is no longer "tender when touched")? Explain.

What are the signs that you still hold bitterness about this wound?

What are signs that you have not fully forgiven the person who gave you this wound?

Have you come to the place where you can love and care for the person who hurt you?

- How am I praying for this person?

- How can I care for this person?

- How am I speaking *to* this person?

- How am I speaking *of* this person?

Have I come to the place where my scar has a story of God's power and presence? If so, what is that story?

 A deep wound will always stay open if we are unable to forgive.

My scar:

Where did this scar originate?

Is this scar still painful, or has it healed (so it is no longer "tender when touched")? Explain.

What are the signs that you still hold bitterness about this wound?

What are signs that you have not fully forgiven the person who gave you this wound?

Have you come to the place where you can love and care for the person who hurt you?

• How am I praying for this person?

• How can I care for this person?

• How am I speaking *to* this person?

- How am I speaking *of* this person?

Have I come to the place where my scar has a story of God's power and presence? If so, what is that story?

 Our scars can be signs of victory, not defeat; while they may be visible, they are not painful anymore.

Never, Never, Never . . . Now!

Pray about one person whom you have had a very hard time forgiving. In honesty, when it comes to this person, bitterness not only has roots in your heart, but it has rented a room and moved in. Forgiveness is not only far away, but you have decided (and possibly said), "I will never, never, never forgive this person." You feel in your heart that if others knew how this person has hurt and shamed you, they would agree that this person should never be forgiven . . . he or she doesn't deserve it! It is time to replace your "never, never, never" with a bold and Spirit-led "now!"

1. Bring this person before the Lord in prayer. Talk with God (again) about what the person did to you—the hurt, the anger, the scars he or she has caused.

2. Ask God to help you see the prison of unforgiveness you are living in.

3. Fix your eyes on the cross of Jesus and remember the grace he extended you while you were still a sinner.

4. Pray to Jesus to show you a new vision of the person who hurt you, a vision of healing and wholeness at the foot of the cross.

5. Ask Jesus to capture this person with true faith and to surround the person with amazing grace.

6. Pray for your heart to soften and change in the coming hours, days, and weeks.

> *You can forgive and still remember.*
> *In fact, you may never forget what happened.*
> *But you can be free of the pain of what*
> *happened because you have forgiven.*

Journal

Use the space provided below to write some reflections on any of the following topics:

- What are ways you have made poor choices in hard times rather than good and life-giving choices? How can you make better choices next time?

- What are ways God can grow and mature you as he walks with you through pain and struggle? How might these lessons never be learned and strong character never be developed if you had not walked with God through deep valleys of pain?

- What are some indicators that bitterness is taking root in your heart? What can you do to pull these roots out and ensure that you live in grace, not the prison of bitterness?

_____

_____

_____

_____

_____

_____

_____

_____

_____

_____

_____

_____

_____

_____

_____

_____

_____

 A whole lot of the journey from shame-filled to shame-free living is getting to the point where we learn to trust God.

Recommended Reading

As you reflect on what God is teaching you through this session, read chapters 9–10 of *Unashamed* by Christine Caine if you haven't already. In preparation for your next session, you might want to read chapter 11.

Session 5

HIGHLY
UNLIKELY

Introduction

Back in the mid 1950s, five friends—all young men in their twenties—decided they wanted to follow Jesus, no matter the cost. They were ready to go where Jesus led them, and that meant they would go anywhere in the world. They had one consuming passion: for the spiritually lost to be found by the amazing grace of Jesus.

So, these men devoted themselves to serious preparation to share the gospel with the Huaorani people in the deepest jungles of South America. They trained to be missionaries. They followed the call to reach a violent and hostile people who had never heard the good news of Jesus. And they were all killed by the very people they had prayed for and longed to reach with God's love, slaughtered on a sandy riverfront in the depths of Ecuador.

But the story does not end there. What happened in the years that followed was even more surprising! One of the men, Jim Elliot, left behind a wife and a daughter. Elisabeth Elliot did not wallow in hatred or root her future in bitterness. She packed up her toddler daughter and traveled to the same remote tribe that had killed her young husband and friends. She entered their world, learned their language, loved them relentlessly, and finally, when she knew enough of their words to speak with clarity, told them who she was . . . the wife of one of the men they had cut down by the riverside.

God used Elisabeth to begin an amazing revival among the Huaorani people. He took a lonely young widow and turned her into a courageous and powerful missionary. Only God can do such a thing! The people God uses for his world-changing purposes are always a surprise. A handful of idealistic twenty-somethings and a lonely widow changed a whole people group in Ecuador. But God can also work through an abused and adopted little girl, an ordinary mom, a woman with a shady past—the broken, abused, abandoned, and a cast of countless others. Ordinary people led by the hands of an extraordinary God can change the world.

 God wants the world to see what he can do through people whose trust is in him alone.

Talk About It

Tell about a person in your life who seemed ordinary from the outside, but in your relationship with this person you saw the extraordinary power of God revealed.

or

Share about one Bible character whose story has impacted your life because he or she was a broken or ordinary person whom God used in a great and surprising way.

> *God has and will always use highly unlikely people to accomplish highly unlikely things for his glory. That means that God can use me and God can use you.*

Video Teaching

Watch the video teaching segment for session five, using the following outline to record anything that stands out to you.

Notes

The tactics of the enemy . . . lies, discouragement, and public shaming

God uses unlikely people

You are not disqualified . . . our functional God uses dysfunctional people

A life-changing shift of focus: from me (what I have done or what has been done to me) to Jesus (what he has done for me)

I am not who I used to be

Examples from Jesus' ancestry . . . a motley crew of sinners

Surprising women in the genealogy of Jesus

    Tamar

    Rahab

    Ruth

The hero of every Bible story

> *There are no perfect people;*
> *there is only a perfect God.*

Video Discussion and Bible Study

1. How can one moment, one thoughtless word, one intentional attack thwart or delay a good work God wants to do through us? If you have had one of those moments in your past, you may want to share how that experience affected you.

 It is so important that we do not allow the words and actions of others, or for that matter, even our own self-talk, to define us or limit our potential.

2. What are ways we can battle against the lies and discouraging words people speak into our lives? How does it help to realize that the enemy of our soul is really the one behind these attacks?

The devil will often attack in the very place that God wants to most use us. Tell about an attack (or series of attacks) you have experienced from the enemy. How can these attacks actually give you clarity about how God might want to work in or through you.

> *The enemy is still extremely gainfully employed*
> *doing what he does best: lying, accusing, and*
> *trying to stop us from fulfilling our God-given*
> *purpose and destiny by stealing, killing, and*
> *destroying the freedom that Jesus came to give us.*

3. What good things might never have happened through your life if you had actually believed the shaming words and demonic lies hurled at you? In what specific and practical ways can you become a person who speaks words of blessing and affirmation to the next generation?

4. **Read** 1 Corinthians 1:26–29. What does the apostle Paul say about the kind of people God calls and uses? Why does God use surprising people to accomplish his will in this world?

Tell about an unlikely person God used in your life. How did the power and grace of God in this person impact your life and reveal the surprising ability of God to use anyone he wants for his glory?

5. **Read** 2 Corinthians 4:7–12. Christine taught about how jars of clay were brittle, common, unimpressive, and utilitarian. There was nothing fancy about a clay jar back in the first century when these words were written. Why do you think God calls us "jars of clay"? What kind of picture is he seeking to paint in our minds?

6. How does God gain greater glory when he does his work through ordinary, imperfect, flawed people? How should this encourage each of us and propel us forward in a willingness to serve God and be used by him, even when we do not feel worthy?

7. The pages of the Bible are covered with stories of imperfect, common, or even rebellious people who were used by God. Think about this hall of infamy:

- *Noah* got drunk and accidentally exposed himself,
- *Abraham* lied about his wife,
- *Sarah* laughed at God and then lied to God about her laughing,
- *Jacob* was a deceiver,
- *Moses* was a murderer,
- *Rahab* was a prostitute,
- *Gideon* was paralyzed by fear,
- *Samson* had lust and anger issues,
- *Eli* failed as a father,
- *David* was an adulterer and a murderer,
- *Solomon* married foreign wives and let his heart turn to idols,
- *Elijah* struggled with depression,
- *Jonah* ran away from God and was angry about God's grace,
- *Peter* denied,
- All the *apostles* ran away in Jesus' time of need,
- *Thomas* doubted,
- *Paul* and *Barnabas* had a ministry conflict and split,
- *Martha* was a workaholic,
- The *Samaritan woman* had five husbands and was living with a guy she was not married to,

- *Barnabas* had compromised the gospel,

- *James* and *John* were prideful and wanted special seats in the kingdom.

And the list goes on. What do you learn about God when you look closely and honestly at the people he used to accomplish his purposes in this world? How does this encourage you, and how might it discourage you?

> **God does not ever call the qualified.**
> **He qualifies the called.**

8. **Read** 1 Peter 2:9–10. What do you learn about yourself, as a follower of Jesus, when you read this amazing and revealing passage? How can Peter, inspired by the Holy Spirit, say these things about us when we know our imperfections, struggles, and frailties?

9. In the genealogy of Jesus recorded in Matthew 1, we find numerous people, including four women, who failed in some way. Why do you think there are so many imperfect people among Jesus' human ancestors? How does their presence give you hope and encouragement as you press past shame into God's plan for your future?

A great way to stop focusing on your past is to start declaring out loud who you are in Christ rather than who you were before Christ.

10. How is your life and future going to be different because of what you learned in this study about living unashamed through the power and grace of Jesus?

Choose to embrace the journey from shame-filled to shame-free living throughout your life so that you will rise up and be all that God has called you to be and to do all that God has called you to do.

Closing Prayer

Spend time in your group praying in any of the following directions:

- Thank God that the thoughtless and harsh words of the past do not have power to shame you today or in your future.

- Thank God for the people who have spoken blessing into your life. Pray that you will be a person who speaks blessing and not curses with your words.

- Thank God that he is not looking for perfect people but those who are available and willing to follow him in the midst of their imperfections.

- Offer your life as a simple jar of clay for God's use and glory.

- Pray for each member of your group to walk into a shame-free future as they follow Jesus and embrace his love and grace.

 God uses imperfect people to work out his perfect plan.

PERSONAL STUDY FOR THE COMING DAYS

Pattern Identification

Christine talked about how she saw patterns in the ways the enemy attacked her. For instance, cancer attacked her throat. A professor told her she would not be a public speaker. These points of attack were against her voice, something God planned to use in great ways for his glory.

List five attacks you have experienced throughout your life that have brought shame and gotten in the way of you fully living for Jesus. These can be from your childhood all the way to today:

1.

2.

3.

4.

5.

Once you have completed your list, look for patterns in how and where the enemy has attacked you. What common themes or patterns do you see?

In light of these themes and patterns, what might you learn about what the enemy is trying to keep you from doing for the glory of God?

Pray about what action you might take to begin doing the very things the enemy has been trying to keep you from doing for months or even years. Record your prayer below:

> *It is a powerful thing to remind yourself and to remind the enemy that you are not who you used to be; you are who God says you are according to the authority of his Word.*

Silence Shame by Speaking Blessing

One of the best ways to counteract shame in our world is through speaking words of blessing. Make a commitment, for the next ten days, to help lift the shame of another person by speaking regular, prayerful, intentional words of blessing to that person. Begin by reading and meditating on some passages that help you understand the power of your words:

The tongue has the power of life and death, and those who love it will eat its fruit. (Proverbs 18:21)

The words of the reckless pierce like a sword, but the tongue of the wise brings healing. (Proverbs 12:18)

Do not let any unwholesome talk come out of your mouths, but only what is helpful for building others up according to their needs, that it may benefit those who listen. (Ephesians 4:29)

Pray about one person in your life who God might want you to bless and encourage. It could be a child, parent, sibling, friend, neighbor, work colleague, a person you know socially, etc. Ask the Lord to put a picture of a face in your mind, a name on your heart, or a deep conviction in your spirit. Write the individual's name below as well as ways you will communicate blessing (face-to-face, on the phone, by text, email, etc.).

Next, write down some specific words of blessing you believe this person needs to hear. These can be words about who she (he) is, her character, the ways you see God alive in her, how you appreciate her, the way she makes a difference in the world around her (whatever you believe will lift up and affirm the person).

At the end of ten days, remember to continue blessing this person and pray about one more person who might need words of encouragement.

Thank You

God has placed people in your life who have been a source of blessing, encouragement, and verbal affirmation. Take time to reflect on at least one such person and what he or she has meant to you. Ponder how God has relieved shame and ministered healing to you through this person. Then, send the person a thank-you. Be specific.

Let him (her) know that, in a critical and shame-filled world, he has been a source of God's blessing, truth, and encouragement. Let him know that God has used him to impact your life in wonderful ways and that he is an example you are trying to follow as you bless other people.

Imperfect People

Christine introduced four women in the family ancestry of Jesus. Take time to study the lives of these imperfect women who God used to accomplish his perfect will by bringing Jesus, the Savior, into the world. Brace yourself; these stories are not pretty nor are they for the faint of heart. But they will teach you that God works through all kinds of people.

Imperfect Person: Tamar

Study: Genesis 38

Study notes and reflections:

Life lessons learned:

Imperfect Person: Rahab

Study: Joshua 2 and 6

Study notes and reflections:

Life lessons learned:

Imperfect Person: Ruth

Study: Ruth 1–4

Study notes and reflections:

Life lessons learned:

Imperfect Person: Bathsheba

Study: 2 Samuel 11

Study notes and reflections:

Life lessons learned:

Daily Proclamation

Sometimes it is healthy and helpful to declare what God's Word says is true. We forget. We believe the lies of the enemy. And, speaking the truth aloud locks into our hearts and minds the reality of God's power and work. Consider reading the following simple declarations aloud every day for the coming thirty days:

- I am FORGIVEN: God has removed my *debts*.

- I am JUSTIFIED: God has totally changed my *state*.

- I am REGENERATED: God has transformed my *heart*.

- I am RECONCILED: God himself has become my *friend*.

- I am ADOPTED: God has changed my *family*.

- I am REDEEMED: God has changed my *ownership*. I am his.

- I am SANCTIFIED: God has changed my *behavior*.

 Choose to believe what God says about you in his Word and to trust that he will somehow make a way where there seems to be no way.

Journal

Use the space provided below to write some reflections on any of the following topics:

- What were some of those shaming moments you faced in a public setting while growing up? What lies did the enemy try to tell you, and how do you need to hear God's truth today?

- What words of blessing and encouragement do the people around you need to hear, and how can you be God's messenger of grace in the lives of those people?

- What truth do you need to lock into your heart so you are always ready to battle the shame-filled lies the enemy seeks to tell you?

_____

_____

_____

_____

_____

_____

_____

_____

_____

 We can do hard things for the glory of God.
The world has declared shame on us, but today
I am decreeing shame off us, in Jesus' name!

Recommended Reading

As you reflect on what God is teaching you through this session, read chapter 11 of *Unashamed* by Christine Caine if you haven't already.

SMALL GROUP LEADER HELPS

To ensure a successful small group experience, read the following information before beginning.

Group Preparation

Whether your small group has been meeting together for years or is gathering for the first time, be sure to designate a consistent time and place to work through the five sessions. Once you establish the when and where of your times together, select a facilitator who will keep discussions on track and an eye on the clock. If you choose to rotate this responsibility, assign the five sessions to their respective facilitators up front so that group members can prepare their thoughts and questions prior to the session they are responsible for leading. Follow the same assignment procedure should your group want to serve any snacks/beverages.

A Note to Facilitators

As facilitator, you are responsible for honoring the agreed-upon time frame of each meeting, for prompting helpful discussion among your group, and for keeping the dialogue equitable by drawing out quieter members and helping more talkative members to remember that others' insights are valued in your group.

You might find it helpful to preview each session's video teaching segment (they range from 19–23 minutes) and then scan the discussion questions and Bible passages that pertain to it, highlighting various questions that you want to be sure to cover during your group's meeting. Ask God in advance of your time together to guide your group's discussion, and then be sensitive to the direction he wishes to lead.

Urge participants to bring their study guide, pen, and a Bible to every gathering. Encourage them to consider buying a copy of the book *Unashamed* by Christine Caine to supplement this study.

Session Format

Each session of the study guide includes the following group components:

- **"Introduction"**—an entrée to the session's topic, which may be read by a volunteer or summarized by the facilitator

- **"Talk About It"**—icebreaker questions that relate to the session topic and invite input from every group member (select one, or use both options if time permits)

- **"Video Teaching"**—an outline of the session's video teaching segment for group members to follow along and take notes if they wish

- **"Video Discussion and Bible Study"**—video-related and Bible exploration questions that reinforce the session content and elicit personal input from every group member

- **"Closing Prayer"**—several prayer cues to guide group members in closing prayer

Additionally, in each session you will find a **"Between-Sessions Personal Study"** section **("Personal Study for the Coming Days"** for session five) that includes a personal reflection, suggestions for personal actions, a journaling opportunity, and recommended reading from the book *Unashamed*.

EVERY 30 SECONDS

somebody is forced into the
bondage of modern-day slavery.
We exist to change that.

_____

Our goal for humanity is simple: Freedom.

Join us as we work to abolish injustice in the 21st century.

A21.org   @A21   @A21   @A21

PROPEL WOMEN

PURPOSE

PASSION

POTENTIAL

For articles, videos and other free resources, visit
www.PropelWomen.org

Unashamed

Drop the Baggage, Pick up Your Freedom, Fulfill Your Destiny

Christine Caine

Shame can take on many forms. It hides in the shadows of the most successful, confident and high-achieving woman who struggles with balancing her work and children, as well as in the heart of the broken, abused and down-trodden woman who has been told that she will never amount to anything. Shame hides in plain sight and can hold us back in ways we do not realize. But Christine Caine wants readers to know something: we can all be free.

"I know. I've been there," writes Christine. "I was schooled in shame. It has been my constant companion from my very earliest memories. I see shame everywhere I look in the world, including in the church. It creeps from heart to heart, growing in shadowy places, feeding on itself so that those struggling with it are too shamed to seek help from shame itself."

In *Unashamed*, Christine reveals the often-hidden consequences of shame—in her own life and the lives of so many Christian women—and invites you to join her in moving from a shame-filled to a shame-free life.

In her passionate and candid style, Christine leads you into God's Word where you will see for yourself how to believe that God is bigger than your mistakes, your inadequacies, your past, and your limitations. He is not only more powerful than anything you've done but also stronger than anything ever done to you. You can deal with your yesterday today, so that you can move on to what God has in store for you tomorrow—a powerful purpose and destiny he wants you to fulfill.

Join the journey. Lay ahold of the power of Jesus Christ today and step into the future—his future for you—a beautiful, full, life-giving future, where you can even become a shame-lifter to others. Live unashamed!

Undaunted

Daring to do what God calls you to do

Christine Caine

Christine Caine is no superhero. She's just like you. And she is changing the world.

Using her own dramatic life story, Christine shows how God rescued her from a life in which she was unnamed, unwanted, and unqualified. She overcame abuse, abandonment, fears, and other challenges to go on a mission of adventure, fueled by faith and filled with love and courage.

Christine offers life-transforming insights about not only how to overcome the trials, wrong turns, and often painful circumstances we all experience, but also how to grow from those experiences and be equipped and empowered to help others.

Her personal stories will inspire you to hear your own name called—just as Christine heard hers—to go into a dark and troubled world. Each of us possesses all it takes to bring hope, create change, and live completely for Christ.

Unstoppable

Running the Race You Were Born To Win

Christine Caine

Each of us has a race to run in life. But this is a different kind of race. It's more than a competition, greater than a sporting event. It's a race with eternal implications—a sprint to destiny.

But many times in our race, we're burdened and intimidated by life's challenges along the way. The task seems too tough, the path too perilous, the race too rigorous.

What if you knew the outcome of the race before it began? What if victory was promised before the starting gun ever sounded? This truth would change the way you live your life—revolutionize the way you run your race.

Slow out of the blocks? *It's okay. Don't give up!*

Trip and fall in the first turn? *Doesn't matter. The race isn't over!*

Disheartened by an unexpected obstacle? *Keep going. You can make it!*

In *Unstoppable*, bestselling author, global evangelist, and human-trafficking activist Christine Caine enthralls us with true stories and eternal principles that inspire us to run the race of our lives, receiving the baton of faith in sync with our team, the body of Christ.

Your race is now. This is your moment. When you run with God in his divine relay, you can't lose. You're running the race you were born to win. It's time to run a new way. It's time to realize ... you are unstoppable.

Available in stores and online!

Living Life Undaunted

365 Readings and Reflections from Christine Caine

Christine Caine

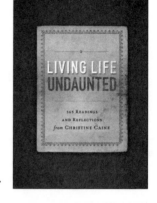

You don't have to be a superhero to change the world. You just have to listen for God calling your name.

Drawing from her bestselling book *Undaunted*, as well as several of her other inspirational writings, author and advocate Christine Caine presents 365 thought-provoking devotionals that will inspire you to overcome your life circumstances, create change, and bring the hope of Christ to a dark and troubled world.

Each daily reading offers the wisdom, encouragement, and companionship you need to begin your own mission of adventure. Even if, like Christine, you began your story unnamed, unwanted, and unqualified, you can be fueled by an unstoppable faith and filled with Christ's relentless love and courage.

The world is waiting. Do you hear God calling your name?

Available in stores and online!

ZONDERVAN®
.com